Whale Song:

Choosing Life with Jonah

Whale Song:

Choosing Life with Jonah

Keren Dibbens-Wyatt

Migiwa Press

2016

First Edition 2016

ISBN: 978-1-326-83708-2

Copyright © Keren Dibbens-Wyatt 2016

All rights reserved. This book or any portion thereof may not be reproduced or used in any manner whatsoever without the express written permission of the publisher except for the use of brief quotations in a book review or scholarly journal.

Keren Dibbens-Wyatt has asserted her moral right to be identified as the author of this work.

Published by Keren Dibbens-Wyatt

Contact for sales and all other enquiries: kerendibbenswyatt@gmail.com

Or visit our websites:

www.kerendibbenswyatt.com

www.stillwatersministries.co.uk

Unless otherwise stated, all Scripture quotations are taken from THE HOLY BIBLE, NEW INTERNATIONAL VERSION®, NIV® Copyright © 1973, 1978, 1984, 2011 by Biblica, Inc.® Used with permission. All rights reserved worldwide.

Scripture quotations marked (ESV)or (ESV®) are from The ESV Bible (The Holy Bible, English Standard Version®) published by Harper Collins Publishers ©2001 by Crossway. Used by permission. All rights reserved.

Cover artwork © by Keren Dibbens-Wyatt all rights reserved

This book is dedicated with gratitude to my parents, Valerie and Graham, for showing me what Love is and helping me to choose Life.

For Susannah

Contents

Introduction	page 11
Time in the Dark	page 15
Fleeing God	page 18
My Story	page 29
Choosing Life	page 41
Down to the Depths	page 46
Rescue	page 51
Time in the Belly	page 54
Rebirth and Prayer	page 63
Singing in the Dark	page 66
The Reluctant Prophet	page 74
A Second Chance	page 81
Scorched	page 85
Disaster and Salvation	page 89
Compassion	page 96
Conclusion	page 100
Questions for Reflection	page 105
Final Prayer	page 109

Introduction

Jonah is one of the shortest books in the Bible, with only four chapters. It tells the story of an Old Testament prophet whom God instructs to go to the city of Nineveh, to prophesy their doom if they do not repent of their wicked ways and turn to God. Nineveh was situated on the east bank of the Tigris River, in what we would now call Iraq (near the present city of Mosul) and was the capital of the Assyrian Empire.

The story takes place sometime during the reign of Hebrew King Jeroboam the Second (786-746 BC), and our hero (or is Jonah one of the first anti-heroes, perhaps?) was from a few miles north of Nazareth in Israel, so the mission God gave him was quite an undertaking, logistically as well as spiritually. Jonah, sure that the compassionate God he knew would relent of the disaster he was threatening on the city of Israel's enemies, and not at all keen on the idea of a long journey which might end in mercy, promptly takes off in the opposite direction, boarding a ship at Joppa, and sailing straight into a horrendous storm.

Thrown into the sea by the ship's crew to quell God's anger, Jonah sinks to the bottom where he cries out to the Lord, who sends a giant fish to swallow him up and bring him safely to shore. The fish is traditionally depicted as a whale, and since Pilot whales do frequent the Mediterranean Sea, they are a likely candidate for the role. Jonah spends three days and nights in the whale, and is then unceremoniously spat up onto the shore, where God asks him again to go to Nineveh.

This time, the prophet goes in full obedience, travelling over five hundred miles to preach the message to his foe that they will be destroyed in forty days. To his horror, it seems, the city repents immediately, and God relents. Jonah sits outside of Nineveh, hoping against hope that God will still punish them. God grows a vine plant to give his prophet shelter from the hot sun, but, in a story within the story, also sends a worm to eat away the vine, so that poor Jonah's bare head gets scorched. Jonah is incensed, and beside himself at what he sees as God's grace extended to his enemies, and his unfairness at taking his own God-given shelter away. The book ends with a meaningful exchange between Jonah and his God about what mercy and compassion really mean, with God having the last word: *"And should not I pity Nineveh, that great city, in which there are more than 120,000 persons who do not know their right hand from their left, and also much cattle?"* (4:11 ESV)

All this, and yet, when we think of Jonah, we are tied to the image of the man who spent time in the belly of a whale. This is the bit that fascinates us and it is something forever linked to his name. We tend not to remember him as the great prophet of God he was certainly regarded as in his day. We generally forget that this is the man who preached what in English would have been an eight-word sermon and which brought an entire city to its knees in repentance. No, when we think of Jonah, we think of a strange, almost comical figure, a man who ran from God and endured the same fate as Pinocchio, being swallowed by a giant sea creature, staying alive in its belly until it coughed him up again.

Because of this, Jonah tends to be either an overlooked prophet or a figure of fun, but I love his honesty and vulnerability and identify with his downright stubbornness. There is far more to this story than a first glance tells us. Jonah's adventure is dramatic of course and much favoured in Sunday school teaching as children respond well to such powerful imagery, but this is not a light tale, rather, it is one that talks honestly about the depths of human experience and the merciful and mighty character of God.

In this small book, we will look at Jonah's time in the giant fish and we will try to think of and answer some pertinent questions. How did he get there? What might it feel like to have been there? Have we ever been anywhere similar? How does he get out? What might he have learned and what can we learn from his experiences? We will also look at the other intriguing elements of this beautifully balanced history, some of which I should like to talk about with reference to my own life story. Life is hard, and most of us have had to tough it out in deep, dark places. Jonah, like so many books of the Bible, far from shying away from this truth, meets it head on, with searing honesty.

Time in the Dark

Not only is Jonah's time in the fish the centre of the narrative for his book, but it is to me representative of all those times in my life when I've felt trapped, or been in a state of complete despair. Those times when there is only me, the darkness and God. This is a powerful recipe in fact, but that's hard to see whilst we are in those depths. I once spent about two years where I felt in that desolate place and then the next ten in the belly of the whale. In fact, I think it was only at the time I began to write this book, another two years on in 2011, that I began to feel it was truly my time to be spat up on the shore and be re-commissioned by the Lord. In my depths I was heartbroken, chronically ill to the point of disability and exhaustion (which I have remained), and for at least two of those years, suicidally depressed.

I was living with my parents through the worst part of my personal depths, but for me, it felt like there was just me and the darkness. I knew somewhere on the periphery that God was about, or rather, I knew that the things I'd been through had not stopped me believing in his existence, but I made the age-old mistake of thinking that if I couldn't *feel* God, then he wasn't around. I know now that God is intimately involved in our lives every second, whether we are aware of his presence or not. He never stops loving us, whether we are believers or not, whether we love him or not. It is not even that Jesus is always standing at the door and knocking, as the popular Holbein painting depicts Revelations 3:20, because that might make us see Jesus as some kind of emotionless, annoyingly persistent doorstep evangelist, and he is not like that. I feel that often he is more likely sitting outside the door on the ground, listening to us cry and weeping himself for our pain. He knows when to knock and when to simply be. For me this verse means that he is always present. He is always waiting for us to turn back to him, ever aware of what we are going through: yet he is never pushy, never arrogant, never full of himself, always open to hearing us. When you consider who he actually is, the person through whom all things were created, the Son of the Living God, that's very humbling.

I wish I had known these things during my darkest times. But though I had kept my faith and I knew that God was there and that I loved him, I couldn't for the life of me see how he could possibly love *me*, when he had allowed such terrible things to happen to me. Another few years later in 2016, as I revisit Jonah's story and my own with a view to publishing this book, hindsight bestows much wisdom and clarity. But when we are down in the dark it is far harder to see what is going on. How do we end up in such places? I will interweave my journey with Jonah's in more detail in a little while. But first let's find out how that Old Testament firebrand ended up in such a pit of despair.

Fleeing God

Jonah ends up in the belly of the giant fish because God had to send it in order to save him from drowning. Jonah was given a prophetic mission from God and he immediately turned tail and ran away from it. He disobeyed, he turned and fled. God was asking him to travel a great distance at a large personal cost to take a message of repentance to a city filled with Israel's enemies. The people of Nineveh were Assyrians and no friends of Jonah. It is not so much the effort requested of him that makes Jonah disobey, but as he later explains, the possibility, indeed the probability, of God favouring that city with his mercy.

"He prayed to the Lord, "Isn't this what I said, Lord, when I was still at home? That is what I tried to forestall by fleeing to Tarshish. I knew that you are a gracious and compassionate God, slow to anger and abounding in love, a God who relents from sending calamity." (Jonah 4:2)

Seeing God's grace poured out for a city of Gentiles is not Jonah's idea of a worthwhile commission.

We can glean from what Jonah says here that he did respond to God's original request in prayer and also that he knew what the end result would be. He was honest with God about his doubts and knew he was putting off the inevitable. So, I intuit that as well as fleeing from this particular assignment, Jonah is essentially fleeing from the compassionate nature of God. It is almost as if he can't quite bring himself to face up to who God really is, what God's mercy really means. It is too much. God's goodness is more than Jonah can take, especially if he must see it poured out on people he perceives as enemies. He knows it, but cannot look upon it. I can't help wanting to compare his attitude to that of Moses, who asked to look on the Lord's goodness and in his gentleness, the Lord gave him all he could cope with seeing – a glimpse – and that from the back.

Perhaps Jonah, who clearly knows God well, sees too much and it frightens him. Certainly, his flight is quite determined and costly. The writer of the book considered it worth mentioning that Jonah boarded the boat *"after paying the fare"*. This tells us that it was all "above board" in human eyes. But it also tells us that Jonah's fleeing was most likely very deliberate and calculated, not a spur of the moment decision. The journey was likely to be a long one and wouldn't have been cheap. Jonah was certainly resolute.

Jonah's disobedience to God also cost the sailors and their masters a great deal. The ship's cargo was lost and I dare say the ship itself needed substantial repairs after coming through a storm that had threatened to break it apart. It might have been a voyage that cost them their lives as well had things gone differently.

As he fled his task, God pursued Jonah, sending a storm after him. Interestingly, Jonah would have happily slept through the storm; the sailors on the other hand, fearing for their own lives, had to rouse the prophet from a deep sleep. They also presumably remember that Jonah has told them he is running away from his God, even as they cast lots which point to his being the culprit. On being questioned he is willing to admit the storm is his fault and volunteers to be thrown overboard. This is quite clearly not normal behaviour! But it could tell us quite a bit about Jonah. He is obviously a prophet, he hears from God, and he knows God well (chapter 4 v 2 that I quoted above is one of the best descriptions of God's character I know) so my guess is simply that despite running away he knows he cannot really escape and that his fate is totally in God's hands.

Jonah disobeys God, but utterly trusts him – how else could he sleep deeply below decks in a storm that threatened to break the ship apart? Either that, or he simply does not care what happens. That would be a mark of deep depression, which I can identify with from experience, but is it that or simply resignation in Jonah's case? Or perhaps we can look at Jonah's later behaviour and conclude that this is a master sulker at work. In all his time on the ship in the storm and even as he is thrown overboard, Jonah does not pray, he does not engage with the Lord, he seems to be in the mother of all strops. Perhaps Jonah is suicidal, perhaps he has given up. Perhaps he cannot see a future that he wants to be part of. He knows that God wants him in Nineveh, he cannot for the life of himself (literally) see the point of going. Why go all that way and make all that effort, to save pagans, the enemies of Israel? He wants no part of it, and yet he knows enough of God to realise that there is no way out except total disobedience quite probably leading to death.

It's impossible to tell Jonah's motives for sure, perhaps it is all these things and more. Even in volunteering to be cast overboard, he is clearly still operating in the prophetic because he knows this will calm the sea and he seems very resigned and matter of fact about it, he appears to care little for his own life: *"Pick me up and throw me into the sea," he replied, "and it will become calm. I know that it is my fault that this great storm has come upon you."* (1:12) Again, this could be a mark of depression, but I am not convinced from the scripture that this is where Jonah is; it is possible that he is simply aware that his running away was futile and that his life and death are in God's hands. For one thing, if he were desperately suicidal, he would more than likely have thrown himself overboard, rather than hidden himself away in the bowels of the boat. Being ready to let the sailors cast him in instead speaks more of someone who has thrown his hands in the air in defeat, rather than someone actively seeking to end his own life. This to me is the difference between someone who wishes they were dead, and someone who decides that they need to be dead: the difference between the deeply depressed and the truly suicidal. To those who have not experienced it, this may seem a subtle distinction, but trust me that there is quite a space between the two. There is a big shift between waking up in the morning and wishing you hadn't, and waking up and actively working out how to end your life that day.

Those of you in the UK may well remember 1st May 1997 when Tony Blair was first voted in to general euphoria. I remember that day too, though for different reasons. I just about walked (this was before my major relapse) up to the polling station dragging along behind my family. It took every ounce of energy to follow them and every grain of determination I had, to not walk into the traffic. I remember that feeling well. I was not just wanting to disappear or not be, I was desperate to end my life. It was a real fight. In the end, it was my compassion for my family that won out. I wanted to end the emotional pain so much, but I couldn't do it in front of them. I don't think it was chance that meant I felt like that on that particular day and whilst my parents and I think both my younger brothers were there. I was not meant to be alone. If I had been out on my own that day, things may have been very different. God's compassion was present in my love for my family, and in theirs for me.

Whether Jonah wanted to end it all as I did that day, or was numbly disassociated from caring about his own life through deep depression, he is anyhow well aware that it is his fault that has caused the storm. Instead of praying to the Lord, in concern for his fellow humans if not for himself, he again evades his responsibility for his own sin and the effect it has on others as well as the responsibility of a prophet of God to implore the Lord for help. We can only speculate on why he needs to be woken from a *"deep sleep"*. Has he stopped caring? Is Jonah still trying to escape even though it might cause his own death and that of others?

When they aren't getting a response from their "gods"(probably the sailors were a group from various different locations, each with their own customs and religion) the Captain realises that there is one person who has not called on *his* God because he is asleep in the bottom of the boat. The sailors are desperate and Jonah is soon "outed" as the culprit by the sailors casting lots. They suspect that he is in some way responsible for the danger. I think that maybe the key to Jonah's character is contained in his own description of himself. The sailors ask him who he is: *"So they asked him, "Tell us, who is responsible for making all this trouble for us? What kind of work do you do? Where do you come from? What is your country? From what people are you?"* (Jonah 1:8)

The prophet defines himself: *He answered, "I am a Hebrew and I worship the Lord, the God of heaven, who made the sea and the dry land."* (1:9) How many of us today would describe ourselves in terms of whom we worship? Even in his desperation to get away from God, even in his deliberate disobedience, even on a ship threatening to break up in a terrible storm, even being thrown back and forth and knowing his life is in imminent danger, Jonah cannot separate his identity from his relationship with the Living God. Who is he? He is one of God's people, a Jew, a worshipper. It is his life's business.

Jonah's description of his God to the sailors terrifies them. We may find this strange, seeped in monotheistic tradition and used as we are to the idea of a creator God who is sovereign. But these men may have been more accustomed to worshipping idols of stone or metal, or fragmented powers, and the idea of this God who made everything and to whom all things belong is alien and frightening. In some ways, we still have the same problem today, even as Christians. Oftentimes we don't want a God who thinks for himself and does things his own way, a God who knows more than we do and is our elder and superior beyond our imagining. Oftentimes we'd prefer a more manageable, controllable god who will act as we desire, in ways that make sense to us. But the great I AM does things his way and this is good and right and as it should be, but yes also, terrifying to our narrow ways of thinking.

To those in our world who worship gods of money, fashion, technology, trends, this all-knowing creator of everything is also strange and terrifying. How often do we describe our God in these large and yet faithfully uncomplicated terms? Mostly if we were asked who we worship, wouldn't we plump for something more conventional? The Christian God, Jesus Christ, Saviour of the world? More about how we see ourselves than how we see him, and quite possibly set in jargon so that those we are speaking to gain no insight? Would our evangelism take on a different character, I wonder, if we described our God as the maker of heaven and earth, and proclaimed ourselves his worshippers?

There is only one listening, hearing God, only one God who answers. When the sailors pray to Him and follow Jonah's instructions, the waters are stilled. The sailors learn that in a crisis, you need a God who is more than an idea, you need a God who is alive and can hear and respond and relate: a living God. From the fact that the Lord hears the prayers of the Gentile sailors, we should be encouraged that the Lord hears those who we might arrogantly deem are not yet his – indeed since we are all his creation we are all his sons and daughters.

Here we might pause for a moment to compare this episode with Jesus' attitude to being on a boat in a great storm. He too, very happily sleeps deeply whilst everyone else panics. But his inner calm proceeds from his faith, from knowing and trusting his Father. He knows that he has been given the authority to calm the wind and the rain.

Now I'll be honest, I am a worrier. The hardest advice Jesus gave for me to follow is "Do not worry." Putting myself in the same situation, would I panic like the sailors with Jonah who didn't know the Living God yet, or the disciples who actually had his Son with them in the boat? How do you think you might react?   I think I might manifest a kind of false calm. I tend to do my panicking inwardly and quietly. I think I might just become very low and frightened, but not run around like a headless chicken. Maybe Jonah was the same, but I suspect his resignation had much more to do with his ultimate trust in God than mine would, despite the fact that Jonah could win prizes for his recalcitrant sulking.

So, our hero ends up being thrown out of the boat (but not until the sailors have tried other solutions and not until they have been converted to faith in God by what has happened) and Jonah sinks down into the depths, even to the very seabed, where he is faced with his own mortality, finally praying to God, and in reply, the Lord provides the great fish to rescue his prophet.

And now is the time when Jonah cannot run any more. Now is the time when he must sit in the darkness and face what he has done and who he is. Now is the time when he discovers, like David in Psalm 139, that there is nowhere we can go to be apart from God:

> *"Where can I go from your Spirit?*
> *Where can I flee from your presence?*
> *If I go up to the heavens, you are there;*
> *if I make my bed in the depths, you are there."*

(Psalm 139:7-8)

And this is also a place that God brings us to today when we need to be there.

Often that place that feels like the end of the world is, bizarre as it may seem, God's way of rescuing us. It may be His way of putting us in a spiritual vice, forcing us to take stock of our lives in order to find our way back to him. We might feel squeezed and in pain. It may be the misery that we need to make us seek out our true source of joy. It may be that our hearts have been utterly broken so that we can then look at the heart's healer and find the one true love of our life, which is always and only ever the Lord.

Of course, that doesn't always follow. Sometimes our lives are blighted by tragedy, heartbreak or accidents and we are being hit by life in a wounded world or sabotaged by the enemy. But these things too God can and will use if we have the sense to give them over to him. A lot of the time, the truth is that we've brought ourselves to the deep, dark places of life. This is not easy to admit, but we all do it. We may have reasons that we fashion into excuses, we may be labouring under terrible hurts, illness or brokenness, usually not of our own making, but we may also still have turned away from God (often because of those very things) in rebellion or stubbornness, even blaming him for them instead of bringing our brokenness to him. Allow me to show you what I mean by telling you a little more of my own story, which I hope will throw some light on my interpretation of Jonah's tale as we go along, and which will weave in and out of our exploration of the narrative.

My Story

I am not afraid, though I may still be ashamed, to say that my lowest points (and they lasted a good number of years) were probably the fruit of my turning away from the Lord. I didn't realise that's what I was doing at the time; but I had previously put my then-husband above God and made his happiness and my identity as a "good" wife, my idol. I had not only let my church life slide, but my prayer life had gone back to being little cries for help every so often, with no real substance as a relationship.

As a very young woman, I had been passionate about God and desperate to serve him. I had had dreams of being involved in ministry and devoting my life to the one I knew as my closest friend and beloved. But when, at nineteen, after my first efforts to find a place in mission abroad were thwarted, worldly love was discovered. This was taken as consolation after my perceived failure, and my first choice faded into the background.

I married at 22, after several years of poor health, failing to recover from a bout of glandular fever. I somehow finished my degree in Literature, and then entered the workplace, doing financial administration, constantly struggling with fatigue.

Early on in my marriage I started to become extremely ill with the neurological disease M.E. (myalgic encephalomyelitis), which stole all my energy and strength, and it became hellish trying to put in a day's work and hold together a home. I could easily use that as an excuse for focussing less on God, but it simply doesn't wash, because I ought to have made the Lord my priority, when things were going well and when things were going badly: he ought to have been my first port of call and not my last resort.

Well now I know as I did not then, that the Lord is the only person who can be our true love, he is the only person who will love us through anything, always forgive us, never let us down, never move away, never die, never betray us, never decide we are not his cup of tea anymore, never move on from us, never grow out of us, and so on.

This truth I learnt, as we often learn truth and as Jonah did too, the hard way. As I became more and more ill, my husband found someone else and one day in April, when I was 26, he sent me away from both him and our home. At the same time, I lost my job and my waning health, and I discovered that even my very identity was shattered, because it had been tied up in the wrong things. I was utterly devastated, and in my heart as well as blaming my former husband, I blamed God. I still loved the Lord, of that I am quite sure. But in that shattered heart, I thought he was the one who ought to have protected me.

Like Jonah, I thought that God ought to have acted the way I wanted Him to, and not according to His own character. He was the one who ought to have made sure I was looked after, who ought to give me a miracle healing, who ought to have protected me from sickness, from heartbreak, from an impending divorce, from being cheated on, from losing my job and my home. And He hadn't, and I had to deal with it and I couldn't.

I was weak, ill and hurting and I did not have a clue what to do with any of it. I wasn't in a position to give any of it to God, though I'm sure I asked Him for help over and over again (and by the way those prayers were answered, but He had to take his time). I couldn't give my hurts to God because I no longer trusted Him to act. You can love someone without really trusting them, and without really knowing who they are. Love can truly be blind. Maybe, like Jonah, I was in the king of all sulks, perhaps without even realising that's what I was doing.

I believe now, as I could not then, that God was at work in all of this. He rescued me by putting me back in the bosom of a very loving family who took care of me. My parents were wonderful, looking after me and my cat. My poor Dad then found himself looking after me as well as my Mum who then also developed a strain of M.E. and who had just lost her own Mum. We muddled along in our broken-hearted mess in a house full of Gran's furniture, my furniture and the debris of a shipwrecked marriage: two broken bodies and one frazzled man, propping one another up and holding on to the only thing we had left: Love.

Self-pity was a huge crutch for me during these years. I was utterly shell-shocked at all the losses and I was so physically ill that I was spending most days lying in bed. M.E. robs you of any stamina, any possibility of exerting yourself, it makes you unbearably weak, and comes with a whole myriad of other unpleasant symptoms, including pain, sleep and digestive disorders, cognitive dysfunction and many others I shan't bore you with, but all of which make life incredibly hard, not least because it takes an age to recover from any kind of exertion (particularly physical). This last fact hit me hard the following spring when I had a major relapse after walking too far and ended up barely able to stand, let alone walk. It was then I got hold of a wheelchair and I still use one today, eighteen years later.

But although losing my walking ability was horrendous, it was before that, during that first year, that I had my darkest times. I could not see the point of life, or at least not of my own life continuing. I felt a burden and a source of misery to everyone (and probably was a lot of the time) and that we would all be better off if I were dead. We've already wondered if that is similar to how Jonah was feeling when he ran from God and waited to be thrown into the raging sea. There are times, for me like the 1st May 1997 as I already described, when the pain is so hard and so loud we cannot see any purpose for our lives.

The following August things were, if possible, worse still. I felt completely empty and pointless, exhausted and if anything, even beyond the crippling emotional pain that I had been going through up to that point. It was like a numbness of soul. I still felt the pain but I no longer wished to be. I sat up in my bed in my parents' living room (poor souls, there was nowhere else to put me just then – what they sacrificed for me and how they suffered!) got myself a glass of water, took a great handful of pills and said to God, "Right, I'm going to do this. If you don't help me or say something by the time I've counted to ten, I'm going to do this." How we plea bargain with God! How we think we should be able to manipulate him. I told you, says Jonah, I knew this is how it would be!

I counted slowly down from ten to one. I felt nothing. God was totally and utterly absent – this is what I felt in my soul. And yet still I believed in him – I knew he was real, but he was not there for me. And there was the crux of my problem. I felt (because I now know this wasn't true) that he was not interested in my life, that he did not love me. I had a very long moment where I felt completely bereft and forsaken. I half-heartedly said zero, I think. I remember closing my hand around the pills, and I suddenly knew that I had made a decision. It was not a blinding flash of inspiration. I did not feel a thing. I certainly felt nothing from God. I was a nothing, a zero (I had literally counted myself down and out after all) and I felt, I knew with total certainty, that I was empty and numb and dead inside, **and that I was going to carry on anyway**. The only motivation I had for this decision – and I'm not entirely sure now looking back how conscious it was – was my parents. I knew that if I killed myself that it would wound them horribly. I couldn't do it. I couldn't put them through it. And I was aware (at least this is what I thought) as I made that decision that I was condemning myself to a lifetime of misery and nothingness. But still I couldn't do it to them.

And so I maintain now, that it was love that saved my life that day. As if to ram home the point, and also to rescue me had I needed it, God sent my Dad into my room a couple of minutes later. I sobbed and showed him the pills in my hand. I don't remember what he said but I do remember the pain on his face. I knew I'd made the right decision. It was the bravest thing I've ever done. It was also the hardest. Like Jonah, trapped and entangled on the seabed, I had faced the possibility of death. Unlike him, it was not so much my upcoming demise that threw my focus back to God, but the largely unconscious realisation that love had to win, that the hope I did not possess had to begin somewhere in denying what I wanted for the sake of sparing someone else.

This episode became a turning point because although later I still felt suicidal, I felt that way in a wanting to fade into the mist or to have never been born kind of a way and never again considered actively doing away with myself. That facing the bottomless pit of emptiness and despair was an epiphany for me and it's why I identify with Jonah's own journey so strongly, and it's why I feel it is right to share it here. Knowing that there was just me and God and that he wasn't going to swoop down and save me from my own pit of self-despair (or at least not in the way I had imagined he would or thought he should) taught me a great deal, whether I could see it at the time or not.

I learned some of the things that I also believe Jonah discovered: that outside of God there is emptiness, numbness; nothing worth having. I learned that the greatest force in the universe is love. And though it took me several years to be able to look back to that day and see God's loving, living presence there, I am certain I was saved by love. By my own love for my parents, by their love for me and by God's love in allowing me to find out things I couldn't have learned any other way. And I know that some of you are reading this saying, yes but surely the point was that God wasn't there for you, why didn't you give up or even become an atheist? And it is true that after this episode I believed that he wasn't there for me for a long time and I didn't understand it and I struggled to trust him for a number of years. But one of the things I learned was this: that self-pity and self-centeredness are barriers to God. They keep us from him. Most of all, they keep us from hearing him.

God's compassion is everlasting and ever reaching and he was there in all his love and compassion that day. But how could I feel or see that when I was so eaten up with my own misery? It was impossible. So he showed his presence in a way I would understand, through my Dad. Maybe my father's appearance that brought love into the room was like Jonah's whale swimming into view, bringing air and rescue to a drowning man.

Looking back now so many years later and trying to make sense of what I felt at that crucial moment is hard, but I do believe that I understood suddenly that God was trusting me to make the right decision, the right choice. I believe he stayed his hand in not speaking to me in a big booming voice because he wanted my decision to carry on, and the reason why, to be utterly my own. It was not easy, as I say it was probably the hardest thing I have ever done, knowing the pain would continue; both physically and emotionally, but it was my choice and that makes it easier to hold to.

This life or death choice is the same one the Lord offers the Israelites in the desert, through Moses, as a multiple choice question, and just in case they are dithering and don't know the answer he helps them out with a clue:

> "This day I call the heavens and the earth as witnesses against you that I have set before you life and death, blessings and curses. Now choose life, so that you and your children may live and that you may love the Lord your God, listen to his voice, and hold fast to him."

(Deuteronomy 30: 19-20)

That wasn't the end of my story of course, and so far it does not have a happy ever after ending. But I'm not expecting one until I go home to meet my Lord. My health improved somewhat and then declined again, and I am now happily remarried, but the most powerful change is in my relationship with God.

I remained bitter for some time until a Christian doctor in General Practice gave me a word that Jesus was waiting for me patiently. Somehow this seeing by someone else melted my stubborn heart and I hurled myself back into the Lord's arms. It was a wonderful reunion and I have never taken my relationship with God for granted again since. I'm sure I have let him down very badly, but have also always held him dear in my heart and found my way back to him. Our love and friendship have developed beyond my wildest hopes since then.

I have spent so many years now in the belly of the great fish, too sick to do much at all, most of the time barely able to walk, stuck in looking at four walls, or at a ceiling for the most part, and yet this is the time that God has used to solidify my faith, to train me to hear his voice, to know his Word better now I can read a little, to come to terms with who I am and am not, who the Lord is, and to give my life, my heart, my self, my time, all more and more utterly up to him every day.

It has been a long, slow process, and one full of pondering, questioning, tears, spiritual consolations and spiritual dryness, turnings away and turnings back. But although it has been incredibly hard, it has also been incredibly rewarding. How else would such a rebellious, self-contained soul have grown close to the Lord?

I am actually at a point now, and it feels strange to write it, where I am able to often (not always!) feel thankful that I have been so ill, because of what the Lord has done with that time, that inability, that enforced stillness, those prayers. He has been crafting me and refining me and there is a very long way to go, but I feel in my spirit that beginning to write about my experiences, and the relationship with the Living God and the things he has had me ponder along the way marks my time of being vomited onto the beach. It's the time of God's commissioning me as finally usable to some degree because of my weakness. It feels like standing on a sandy shore as the prophet Jonah must have done, shivering in fish bile and perhaps rather bewildered but determined to serve.

I have not been healed of my M.E. yet, but I am well enough to write a little now and again. I pray this will be a new adventure, used of God and that it will bless others. I pray it will give hope to those down in the depths and those in the bellies of whales, and that it will help them make some sense of the small, dark world in which they find themselves.

Of course, it all comes down to faith in the end and I think the bottom line for me was that at the end of my misery, at the end of the line and the bottom of the pit, in the very depths of my own personal ocean of misery, was freedom. I felt most clearly of all that the decision was utterly mine; that I had been given the power to choose: life or death. That this was a precious choice, a hard-won choice, a choice given me out of love and respect and that I was being trusted with it. Jonah too, gets to a point where he makes that choice, as we shall see shortly.

Even as I write this though, I am aware that honesty is hugely important and I need to also make it clear that there are days, like today in actual fact, where I feel so ill, pointless, physically empty and exhausted, that I find it hard to be thankful for anything at all, let alone for how God has used this terrible sickness. But on these days I make a point of choosing to thank him anyway, of choosing to hold onto my Lord. It is a little like making that big choice to live all over again, and often it is very hard. But it is a choice I make daily, sometimes in joy and sometimes through gritted teeth or tears of exhaustion and pain. But it's my choice. As for me and my house, we will serve the Lord.

Choosing Life

It is this experience of being given the strength to choose not to commit suicide that heightens my compassion for anyone suffering, and my determination to come at life with a positive frame of mind. Every life is worthwhile in some way; everyone is potentially whole. Mother Julian of Norwich's locution that "All shall be well, and all shall be well, and all manner of things shall be well," expresses a deep truth to me, that everything is redeemable. Compassion and non-judgement seem part and parcel of this understanding. I would never condemn someone who had committed or attempted to commit suicide, but I would categorically say that it is ever God's plan. I have got bucket loads of empathy however, for anyone in that much physical or emotional turmoil. I also believe that Jesus does too and more so of course. No-one understands pain the way he does, in humility, without judgment and with total comprehension and empathy; for who has suffered more than he?

A friend of mine had a daughter with post-traumatic stress disorder who after years of fighting pain and horrific flashbacks of a terrible event, came to the decision to take her own life. On hearing of her death, I prayed for the whole family later the same night. In the morning on waking I had a powerful picture imprinted on my mind. I saw a young woman in terrible pain entering a dark tunnel and Jesus coming alongside her. He spoke loving kindness to her, she put her head on his shoulder and they then started to walk towards a great source of light at the end of the tunnel, Jesus speaking love and understanding to her the whole way. As they walked, she was coming to trust him more and more.

I believe the Lord can and does do wonders with those last few moments of life, that he can stretch them out to be whatever a person needs. Suicide is never a good thing; it is contrary to God's plans. Life is a gift from Him and it is only His to take away. But yes, I do believe that Jesus is the King of compassion and understanding and that he always sees our wounds and seeks to heal them and he knows where they have led us.

This picture taught me that the Lord's love reaches places I had not considered it could; that there is always hope even for the darkest pain, and that we should never ever stop praying for anyone.

I believe also at the end of the day from both this, the scriptures and my own experience that it is love that saves us from such a fate as suicide, and that it is most particularly the loving of others instead of ourselves, the focus being consciously put onto God and onto our brothers and sisters in humanity that forces us out of our own pain. This is I believe also the way forward when we are caught in the pain of self-loathing or self-harming. If we are looking into our own selves all the time we end up like Kurtz in Conrad's Heart of Darkness and see only the worst horrors; horrors only God can transform. Looking towards him and to the needs of other people is the first step back to balance. Perhaps Jonah could identify with this, having faced his own personal abyss at the bottom of the sea, seeing there only darkness and death until he turns his heart back to the Lord, the source of light and life.

God's commands are always for our own good, even when to some people they seem draconian. God commands us to love Him with all our hearts, minds and strength not only because it is the right thing to do, but because it will do us nothing but good! Putting ourselves at the centre of the universe leads to dark places, lies and pain. Self-centredness steals our joy and even our very breath. Choosing his own way instead of God's leads Jonah right into a confrontation with his own mortality. At the bottom of the sea he sees the truth that there is only one way to look for life and that is not further into the darkness, but upwards to the light. *"Yet I will look again towards your holy temple......and my prayer rose to you, to your holy temple."* (chapter 2 verses 4 and 7 –partial).

Choosing life means choosing a non-judgmental way of life and it means choosing God and it means choosing love. In short, we need to find positive reasons for continuing and they need to be altruistic. Selfishness will only lead to dark places and misery because it focuses us in on ourselves where there is nothing ultimately good to sustain us. Don't misunderstand me, for I know that we are good in as much as the Lord pronounced us so as his creation and in the ways we are made in his image, just that any goodness in us needs to point us towards the source of that goodness, the Lord, and anything positive in us is merely a reflection of Him. Even Jesus refused to call himself good in comparison with the Father. There is nothing solely of ourselves that will give us sustenance.

Nor do I mean that depression or feeling suicidal are expressions of selfishness. Like grief or trauma, they are about the very deepest pain that human beings can experience, and should arouse all our compassion.

In short, focusing on ourselves brings death, focusing on God brings life. The breath of God is our very life force and His Word is what upholds us. It was the Word of God made incarnate in Jesus Christ who achieved the ultimate victory over death and who brings us life in all its fullness. It was His engagement with the darkness on the cross and in the belly of His own whale, entombed in death for three days and nights, just like Jonah, that facing of death and his victory over it that passes on to each Christian the precious gift of life.

If Jesus had to experience His own time in the belly of the whale, bringing life out of death, then we, in sharing His life and sufferings, should expect to encounter those fish-gullet experiences in our own lives as we reflect his. We will get dark nights of the soul; but we also hold the keys to victory, hard won by our Lord.

Choosing life is also about what we let into our lives and about how we deal with what arrives unbidden; and learning to recognise each for what they are; bringing both to God as only He can transform it all. Faith and trust are always the catalysts for transformation and renewal.

Down to the Depths

Jonah, like many of us, only chooses life when he is faced with death. Until that point, the God-given purpose of his life is something he is more than happy NOT to choose, thank you very much. There is even something of the death wish about the way he seems to volunteer to be thrown into the water to save the ship. He has to be facing the imminence of the end of himself before he can really make the choice that he needs to.

God allows Jonah to sink right to the bottom of the sea, he is actually on the seabed, *"the earth beneath barred me in forever"* before God sends the giant fish to rescue him. God could have provided the fish to catch Jonah at the surface of the water, or a dolphin perhaps for him to ride on and take him to safety. Crucially though, Jonah doesn't ask for God's help until much later, when he is at the bottom of the ocean. As we noted before, Jonah doesn't engage with God whilst on the ship and seems resigned to be thrown overboard rather than accept his commission. Jonah is allowed by the Lord to make his choice, and until the point where he is face to face with physical death and indeed with spiritual death (which we often define as separation from God), then death is indeed what he chooses. Never does the possibility of life seem so desirable as when it is almost taken from us, then it is a heart cry, a shout from somewhere deep down in our darkness that cries out for life, as something in me once did.

God allows Jonah to get eyeball to eyeball with his choice, he allows him to sink and nearly drown. Before he can be used, Jonah must acknowledge his need for God. Jonah needs to see and experience the depths. It takes a taste of the depths to make him cry out to the Lord and to remember who God is. Jonah doesn't mince his words about the experience. Like King David, he is completely honest about the pain and despair, the horror and the hopelessness, the feeling of being utterly alone deep down in the depths. I have heard the accounts of people who have nearly drowned and it sounds an elongated and extremely painful process.

If we take the fall of Jonah down to the bottom of the sea as a metaphor for our own dark times, there are a great many parallels. In the worst times we can feel that we have been thrown overboard into a raging tempest. We can feel bashed and knocked about and engulfed by waves and currents. Everything feels out of our control and we are swept under. We are fearful; feeling surrounded and trapped. I am always particularly struck by Jonah's description in verses 5 and 6 that there was seaweed *"wrapped around my head"* and that he felt that he had sunk down to *"the roots of the mountains"*. How often in our own despair and separation from God do we feel that we are falling into death, that there is no air left for us to breathe, that we are banished from God's sight, that we have sunk down and have come to the lowest point possible, that there is no way out, that we are *"barred...in forever"* (Jonah 2:6)? This would be a very good description of how it feels to be suicidal as well as how it feels to be facing anything that feels like a dead end, including death itself.

Jonah does actually reach a point very close to death, and finally he prays to the Lord as his *"life was ebbing away"* (Jonah 2:7) This is the crux point, the moment at which God is acknowledged again by Jonah as being his Lord and the author of life, more particularly as his saviour. In his prayer, Jonah finishes with the truth he has learned so painfully at this point, *"Salvation comes from the Lord."* (Jonah 2:9) But as described in his prayer, this is also the point at which Jonah chooses life over death. He could drown in his own stubbornness but he prays instead. It is always, always, *always* the right thing to do to pray and never to give up hope, even when all seems hopeless. Even when you are about to drown on the seabed, entangled in weeds and trapped by the depths weighing down on you and the lowest point possible beneath you, it is not too late to pray. If we cry out to the Lord in our pain, he hears us. It may just be the word "help" or a cry from the heart. Jonah's lungs would have been burning up with pain and he would have been utterly incapable of speech at this point so his prayer must have been an inner cry.

This said, we must remember that God won't respond to emotional blackmail – I tried that myself in my worst moment as I described – "if you don't act, I'll do this." But he is the ever-listening, always compassionate King of mercy, our God. If we cry out, if we call to the Lord in our distress, as Jonah did, then he will answer, he will listen to our cry. I sometimes wonder at the fact too, that the Lord must have had faith in me to call out and make the right choice, as he certainly did with Jonah.

Jonah describes the various stages of his torment in detail. It is about being engulfed, threatened, swept over, surrounded, entangled and trapped. He ends up in a situation that is scary and totally out of his control, where he is totally beyond his capacity to save himself. The seaweed wrapped around his head speaks to us of panic, of the tentacles of the deep places enclosing him, holding him and keeping his body and maybe even his mind. Perhaps he could not even see at this point. This is the ultimate near death experience. This is a place of fear, panic, no hope and crucially of no breath – God's breath is the source of our life and Jonah is without it.

Jonah ends up experiencing a kind of reversal, a photographic negative of how life on dry land looks, he is on ground but it is the seabed and the waters above are not the skies but the sea. His fate is about ending up somewhere he was never built to be and needing a rescuer; much as we were not built to be far from God, separated from him by our sin and lack of his breath and needing Jesus to come to our rescue.

Rescue

In terms of depression of course, not that many of us can say that we have experienced a cure or a complete healing. Usually, these deep and difficult places leave us with scars, some of them physical, most unseen. But those of us who have survived these times, particularly those where circumstances seemed to have hounded us to these places, or where we feel we escaped by the skin of our teeth, or were rescued (as I feel I was) by love, can look back with hindsight and know that we have come a long way, and that things are not how they used to be. We can say we have experienced some measure of healing grace, though it probably differs for everyone.

Depression is a difficult beast to overcome and for most of us, it will be a lifelong struggle to tame it. I do not believe that being a Christian means you do not experience, live and suffer with depression. Indeed, some of the bravest and most whole souls I know do just that. As with physical chronic illness, it is not about how much faith you have, for God chooses to heal us in different ways, and just because one person receives a more tangible miracle for all to see, does not mean another does not receive a blessing of daily grace to get through their lives, tormented by thorns in their flesh. I find it deeply self-righteous and damaging when Christians judge one another by how "healthy" they deem one another to be. Our prayers are answered in different ways, and the only thing to remember is that each rescue has its own pattern, since we are each of us uniquely loved by our Father.

How did Jonah expect God to answer his prayers, I wonder? Probably not by his sending a giant fish to swallow him up I should think! God's solutions are nearly always different to the ones we imagine for ourselves or even the ones we ask for. This is a good thing because crucially He knows best. Now Jonah had sense enough to realise that the fish was a saving grace. This seems to remain true even during his time in the belly of the creature, when he could have despaired again, or thought, what now? How do I get out of this one? Isn't this going from the frying pan into the fire? But he was alive and the Lord had saved him and that was good enough. It was good enough to bring a song of thanksgiving from his lips and to elicit some kind of vow:

"But I, with shouts of grateful praise,
will sacrifice to you.
What I have vowed I will make good."
I will say, 'Salvation comes from the Lord.'" (Jonah 2: 9)

And though we are not privy to its nature we can probably assume his promise may be something to do with being more obedient in the future, especially as he does then go to Nineveh.

A lot of us make the mistake of not recognising the saving graces sent us by God, mostly because they were not what we expected, or more to the point, not what WE would have done in God's place. But thankfully, we are not God. He always does the right thing, the best thing. For Jonah, it was sending a giant fish. Who knows why? Perhaps it was the only way to get to Jonah in time before he drowned, bringing a pocket of air right down to the depths. Maybe it prevented Jonah suffering with the bends, since he would have needed to come up slowly from such a depth. Perhaps it was also because it was a dramatic gesture that might finally get through to Jonah how loved he was, and perhaps it was because God knew Jonah and he were not finished yet and his prophet needed some time with just his God and the dark.

Time in the Belly

Perhaps the greatest reason for God rescuing Jonah in the way he did was because the prophet needed to really experience that death to rebirth scenario, a womb-like experience. It is after all in the womb where God knits us together:

> *"For you created my inmost being;*
> *you knit me together in my mother's womb."* (Psalm 139:13)

Salvation brings with it the possibility of being re-knit, being re-formed in those areas where we need to be. God's reasons were probably all these and more. Certainly, during his time in the fish, Jonah has time to consider all that has happened, make sense of it and form it into the wonderful prayer that we shall look at in more detail shortly.

Most of us in the bellies of our giant fish, don't recognise where we are. We certainly don't recognise God's part in putting us there or even see what has happened as a rescue, or that we might need some time to recover from our ordeal. Or at least, we don't see these things at first. Hindsight is far clearer when we are trying to make sense of our spiritual journeys.

Jonah has more sense. In fact, there is a Job-like quality to his thinking in the whale. In his prayer he acknowledges both the fact that it was God that hurled him into the deep in the first place AND that it was God that saved him and *"brought my life up from the pit,"* and at first glance that seems illogical, but it makes sense with God, who is God and may do as He pleases. But it is not only an acknowledgement of God's utter sovereignty, but also of His goodness. Jonah knows all of this is ultimately for good, he knows it was his own stubbornness and disobedience that got him thrown into the sea and that it was God's mercy that rescued him. He sees God's processes at work. Was there any time at which he wondered if this was a new and different kind of death? Was he to be digested instead of drowned? Sometimes we might feel as though God has caught us from the frying pan only to throw us into the fire, but we need to trust that there are reasons for his mysterious ways. With Jonah, as for most of us, the majority of these insights come later on, not necessarily during our time in the belly of the whale, but probably later still, after we have been regurgitated back into the world. During his worst time of distress at the bottom of the sea, all Jonah did was to call for help, to remember God and pray. Jonah gets *"barred in"* by geography (2:6) ; Job, feels *"hedged in"* by God.

> *"Why is life given to a man*
> *whose way is hidden,*
> *whom God has hedged in?"* (Job 3:23)

The sense of being trapped for our own good is a biblical precedent it is sometimes wise to remember; it can stem panic and feed hope.

Time in the belly, when we get there, is time for prayer. Time for relating to God. Prayer is what causes transformation and rebirth in powerful ways.

My own experience of belly time has certainly been a re-forging. God has gradually led me out of my own selfish bitterness, invited me away from my own pity party, and out into the freedom of obeying him. Ironically this can only happen when we are trapped. Insurmountable circumstances, difficulties that we have no control over, are things which drive us back into the arms of our Maker.

We gradually start to see our own smallness, our own weakness, the impossibility of holding everything together by ourselves. We start to acknowledge the need for someone or something bigger and wiser than we are. We see, like the writer of Proverbs, that all else is meaningless. We start to grasp that riches and accolades and status are pointless pursuits. They might make earthly life a lot more bearable in terms of comforts, but with an eternal perspective, the light of which we begin to learn to see things by in the darkness, they are unimportant.

Essentially, it is in the darkness that we begin to see. It is in the cramped spaces that we start to spread our spiritual wings. It is here, crouched in the belly of a whale, or confined to a sick room, or to a wheelchair, or to life with a difficult family, or to a prison cell, or held in the heartbreak of betrayal or bereavement, that we encounter the Living God. This is partly because there is nowhere else to run, it is partly because our pain forces us to either turn inwards (which leads to bitterness and regret) or outwards.

The being hedged in, the barriers, the failure, the inability to be what we thought we were meant to be, becomes the very thing that helps us to understand that there is more purpose here than we imagined.

It is not on the seabed where Jonah processes what's happened to him, but in the whale. This is where he wrestles with his past and with his ideas about God. This is where he speaks (or sings) his prayer. *"From inside the fish Jonah prayed to the Lord his God."* (Jonah 2:1)

For me too, this period after the depths is the place and time where the process of change began to take root. The drama of going down to the deepest place is too desperate and difficult, it is a turning point, a decision point. Belly time, true dialogue with God is what happens after the rescue. This is where, like Jacob, we are renamed by the Lord after our initial struggle. This is our new spiritual formation, the beginning of the honing and refining of who we are in God.

And it may well be in our lives that we have one dramatic turning point, but you can guarantee that there will be many smaller ones too, for relationship with God is about constant change – ours, not His. It can feel like a series of pendulum swings, where we are always moving away from holiness and then seeing this and turning back to Him. But the swings (if we are focussed on God) become smaller and smaller, though the more we love God, the bigger the distance seems, the greater the fall looks. At the same time, the more intimate the relationship, the easier it becomes to turn back to his love, and to recognise the process for what it is rather than becoming anxious about it.

God's love is always about transformation. He is always moving us forward (sometimes it feels like two steps back and one forward) and bringing us to wholeness, performing a restorative, refining work. As we seek to co-operate with the Lord in this time, we will be constantly renewing our choice for life, constantly having to re-give our yes to God.

Choosing life is about choosing God, letting Him in, allowing Him to work. It is about acknowledgment of his sovereignty in your life, about trusting Him, about faith without seeing, about admitting that we have nothing worth giving and giving it anyway. In this sense the process begun in our time in the belly will last the rest of our earthly life. I believe that this process of change which St Paul calls being changed from glory to glory (2 Cor 3:18), is also what he means when he talks about the working out of our salvation (Philippians 2:12).

We might look at our description here of time in the belly as very much like the dark night of the soul that St John of the Cross famously described, or equate it with testing times such as those experienced by Job on his ash heap or Daniel in the den of lions, Noah building his ark for so many years, or Jesus in the wilderness. In my own understanding, these are not all of the same mould. Job's illness lasted a good while, possibly years, and this could maybe be seen as a qualification for belly time, but my definition of time in the belly, the experience of Jonah as it relates to others, is that it is more a time of quiet reflection, realisation, a cloistering, leading to prayer, restored relationship with God and then on to a second chance, a rebirthing, a new way forward, as opposed to a time of testing, trial or temptation.

Time in the belly is not about those things, though the bastions of self and ego faced in the depths are then further broken down and the process of change begun. Jonah certainly doesn't come out of the whale a changed person, he is as selfish as he was before, but he does have a greater obedience, it is a time of consolidation perhaps, of forced reflection, particularly on the eternal perspective – that God is God, not us, and he is the centre of the universe, not us. This can take a long time to sink in for some of us.

On the whole, I would imagine that Jonah's dark night of the soul happens in his fleeing God, in his trip on the boat, the storm and his sinking to the depths and facing his own mortality.

Moses is perhaps a pertinent example to help us here, because his story can be interpreted in several ways. There's a great deal of subjectivity in how we describe elements of the spiritual journey, particularly as no two people tread the same path and it really comes down to your own understanding (and probably your own experience) of spiritual consolations or aridity, of the dark night of the soul and of your own time in the belly of the whale.

Moses, aged forty, understands that he is to help free the Hebrew people, but thinks it needs to be done from his privileged position in the palace and that it can be done passionately and violently (Acts 7:22-29). After being found out for committing murder, I believe he was most likely in a desperate state, feeling abandoned by God, confused and in spiritual darkness. I would call that period his dark night of the soul. But he then spent forty years in the desert as a shepherd. It would be as a shepherd that he would truly mirror God's character and lead the people of Israel. His time learning who he was, processing his mistake, becoming who God meant him to be, re-forging attitudes, particularly of humility, this I would call time in the belly of the whale.

It is after a period of such time, that we find we have become useable, where we were not before. God can then give us our commissions in life, just as he does to Moses at the site of the burning bush, and just as he does to Jonah, both men having come through a time of recalibration to take on the orders they originally fled from or took on too zealously. Indeed it is very often more a re-commissioning. God saying lovingly, okay, we tried it your way, and look what happened. Perhaps now your failure has given you the necessary humility and we might try it my way. We might note at this juncture that Moses was, at forty, *"powerful in speech..."* (Acts 7:22) and yet at the time of the burning bush forty years later:

"Moses said to the LORD, "Pardon your servant, Lord. I have never been eloquent, neither in the past nor since you have

spoken to your servant. I am slow of speech and tongue."
(Exodus 4:10)

Surprising isn't it, which version of Moses is most useful to God?

Some writers, thinkers and theologians would call all of this time the dark night of the soul. Perhaps belly time is one phase within that, I just find it helpful to think of it as womb time, reknitting, remaking time. It is the place of spiritual rebirth and I don't consider it a time of spiritual dryness, but of spiritual process.

Time in the belly of the whale then, is where we start to make sense of our experiences and let God bring order out of the chaos of our lives, hearts and thoughts, and it comes only after we have been down to the depths. Belly time is hard and it can take many years, but it is where we write our songs and collate and collect ourselves in relation to God.

Rebirth and Prayer

Jonah was in the fish for three days and three nights. This is a biblical time frame we see elsewhere, most notably the time from Jesus' death to his resurrection, and also the time after Saul's conversion during which he was blind. Three days is also the time it takes to visit Nineveh and these instances have interesting parallels. It is the time taken to conquer death and set all its captives free, also the time it takes God's prophet to enter a pagan city and bring it to its knees. It is the time both in Saul and Jonah's lives that they take in darkness after a point of conversion. It is a time then, for the gestation of faith, for cementing a change of heart.

There is a great parallel of course in the story of Jonah, not only to Jesus' death and resurrection – he himself called it the sign of Jonah – but also to the experience of being spiritually born again that Jesus describes to Nicodemus in the gospel of St. John. In becoming Christians, in embracing the Lord's victory, we too experience a death and rebirth. This picture then continues with us in our Christian journey as we constantly die to self, more and more each day, and become birthed more and more like Christ as we do so. The belly of the whale is a womb where we can be reformed and become ready to be reborn, or as in Jonah's case, vomited out onto the land! Either way it is a powerful symbol of a new beginning from a place of confinement, of life brought forth from death, hope from despair, freedom from incarceration. We might even consider Jesus' ministry as well as his death a belly time in terms of our salvation history, in that it started the movement from the old covenant to the birthing of the new.

Central to all of this is the point that it is prayer, that is, relationship and encounter with God, that moves the process on. All we know about Jonah's time in the whale is contained in the prayer recorded, which is mainly about what happened before Jonah was rescued. So in the whale, Jonah was focussing on and processing what had happened to him in the depths.

There is a kind of prayer called the prayer of travail which is often likened to labour pains because it feels like a birthing, a bringing into the earthly realm from the spiritual realm, and also because it is painful, a process of tears and shouts and cries and stamping. But all intercessory prayer, whether for ourselves or others, involves a process of conception, labour and birth, whether we are aware of it or not, and in our own spiritual lives, our journey to becoming more Christ like, our choosing of life over death, choosing God over ego, is a constant circle of labour and birth being played out over and over again.

We ask God for something, our prayer rises to him, it is conceptual, something that's been thought of; God acts, often by speaking, and brings life, brings beginning to the concept, and the process of growing something in the spiritual kingdom of God that will be birthed into the world, is begun.

James spoke of this process as it also applies in terms of evil:

"Then, after desire has conceived, it gives birth to sin; and sin, when it is full-grown, gives birth to death." (James 1:15)

Jesus often talked of the process of the kingdom of God being like earthly processes of growth, just like in the Parable of the Sower:

Others, like seed sown on good soil, hear the word, accept it, and produce a crop—some thirty, some sixty, some a hundred times what was sown." (Mark 4:20)

If we find ourselves becoming attuned to the will of God in our prayer lives, we can be partners with him in truly bringing His kingdom into this one, and this is a large part of the work of the believer, along with proclaiming this new kingdom.

Singing in the dark

So, let us look more closely at Jonah's prayer of gratitude. Jonah's "prayer" and it is called that in most bibles, is in my opinion, a song. I like to think of it as whale song, hence the title of this book. It is more of a psalm than a prayer, though of course, we could equally call the Psalms, prayers. In it, Jonah mostly describes what happened to him. But it not only reads like a psalm of David, with its images of being rescued from the pit and of being heard by the Lord in a time of distress, Jonah even quotes Psalm 42 within it – half of verse seven:

"..all your waves and breakers have swept over me." Is almost exactly the same as the end of Jonah 2, verse 3.

The essence of Psalm 42 is of a longing for God in desperate circumstances. No wonder Jonah feels the urge to quote it and make its imagery his own.

"From inside the fish Jonah prayed to the Lord his God. He said:

"In my distress I called to the Lord,
and he answered me.
From deep in the realm of the dead I called for help,
and you listened to my cry.

You hurled me into the depths,
into the very heart of the seas,
and the currents swirled about me;
all your waves and breakers
swept over me.
I said, 'I have been banished
from your sight;
yet I will look again
toward your holy temple.'
The engulfing waters threatened me,
the deep surrounded me;
seaweed was wrapped around my head.
To the roots of the mountains I sank down;
the earth beneath barred me in forever.
But you, Lord my God,
brought my life up from the pit.

"When my life was ebbing away,
I remembered you, Lord,
and my prayer rose to you,
to your holy temple.

"Those who cling to worthless idols
turn away from God's love for them.
But I, with shouts of grateful praise,
will sacrifice to you.

*What I have vowed I will make good.
I will say, 'Salvation comes from the Lord.'"*

And the Lord commanded the fish, and it vomited Jonah onto dry land."

(Jonah 2:2-10)

The very first statement is one of redemption and fulfilled hope, strikingly like many Psalms; I called Lord, and you answered. Jonah then goes on to describe his horrible ordeal in detail, starting with what happened after he was thrown overboard. Rather than blaming the sailors or himself for this, Jonah gives credit to God for being in total charge of his destiny. He acknowledges God's sovereign actions even when they have horrendous consequences for his servant (albeit his disobedient servant) *"You hurled me into the deep.."* and he also acknowledges God's creation and His sovereignty over the waves of the ocean *"all **your** waves and breakers swept over me"* (my emphasis). Jonah sees his fate as God-given and as a banishment. His primary concern is not drowning, but being put out of God's sight. This, he understands as someone who has experienced a close relationship with the Lord, is the worst outcome possible. Yet even in accepting this fate he is not without hope.

Jonah's response to feeling he is being put out of God's sight is to determine to keep God in his own sights *"yet I will look again toward your holy temple."* The root of this hope, is, I believe, Jonah's knowledge of God's character, as displayed in chapter 4 v 2. *"I knew that you are....a God who relents from sending calamity"* Jonah is well versed in the mercy of God, his awareness of it is the reason he didn't want to go to Nineveh. He knew the mercy of God might make him look foolish.

Towards the end of his prayer, there is a sense that Jonah betrays again his lack of compassion for pagans in comparing himself favourably to those on who worship idols (verses 8-9)– perhaps thinking of those he's just left on the ship or those in Nineveh. He is glad of his own salvation and that is enough to make his heart sing to the Lord and to give his vow of obedience.

Jonah acknowledges in his song that the Lord is the author of salvation and I feel he is not just talking about his current and expedient salvation from drowning, but from death on a deeper level. He knows, as does the psalmist whom he echoes, that this is not just about being saved once from death, but once for all from death even when it claims us.

Also as in the Psalms, the emphasis is on a cry for help that has been answered, a call that is heard. The repeated pattern is always – I'm in distress BUT the Lord has answered or *will* answer me.

The way we experience the story of fall and redemption is that the Lord seemingly forsakes and then finds us again, and it is all for our own good, a painful learning curve indeed! Of course we feel this is what is happening, a spiritual death or separation from God needing an act of restoration. This was also the story of Adam and Eve in the garden at the beginning of things. It is important to note in that story, as it reflects its truth on ours, that God himself never abandoned his children. We moved away from him by our disobedience. He comes calling for us in the cool of the evening, clothes our shame and already has in motion the plan that will bring restored union.

Even Jesus on the cross had this experience of ultimate abandonment that perhaps we might more properly define (as opposed to the concept of belly time already discussed) as the dark night of the soul, even though he had never turned away from his Father. I am no schooled theologian, but my understanding of this is that Jesus carried all our pain, sin and darkness on the cross. I have read and heard it preached that it was God's justice that needed satisfying and that this sin caused a separation here, that God, being all goodness and holiness could not look upon such wickedness, even borne as it was by an innocent. Yet I humbly disagree with this explanation. I believe that God was right there with his beloved Son and never distanced himself. I believe that it was Jesus' perception that changed. He could no longer sense God's nearness or goodness, because the pain he carried was too loud and too heavy. I believe this is the case in all experiences of the dark night. That we are so clouded in darkness, in misery and in pain, in the suffering, in the seeming lack of God, that we feel abandoned, or construe that he must have withdrawn from us in some way, when he has not.

I believe this because of my own experience, but also because of God's compassion, particularly as it is shown to Adam and Eve. God's first act when they sin is to search for them and then to take care of them by clothing them. The Father has to banish them from the Garden for their own good (they must not eat of the fruit of the Tree of Life and become immortal in their now sinful state) but he only acts out of love and never from coldness or judgment. This I also believe because it is the Father that Jesus showed us, who never changes. He never acted in judgment towards sinners but always with compassion, healing and merciful forgiveness.

During this dark night, this perceived abandonment, we make a choice. We can stay where we are or we can choose to have faith, to believe in what is unseen and unfelt. We make a decision to believe that God is there with us because of who he says he is. And once we have done this, we can move on. Jesus, as always, shows us the way. *"Into your hands I commit my spirit."* (Luke 23:46). I cannot sense you, we say, but I give you all of myself anyway. It is, I also believe, imperative that Jesus went through our deepest darkness, including this feeling of abandonment, because how else could he redeem it and show us the way out? It is worth noting too that the darkness that came over the land during the crucifixion lasted from the sixth hour to the ninth hour (Luke 23:44) a three hour period being both a shadow and an echo of the three day experiences of Jonah, Jesus and Saul.

There is always a nadir before there is a zenith it seems, but if there is no movement away from God there is no triumphant return to him. Walking constantly with God is the ideal for which we were created, yet this earthly life seems characterized by the constant of turning, to and from God; but the good news is we often learn to make those pendulum swings we mentioned before shorter and shorter and return home more quickly each time we leave.

The prodigal son cannot return to be wrapped in the Father's cloak of love if he never leaves home. So we find the central core of many biblical stories, and perhaps even of the whole Bible, maybe even the story of the entire human race – a leaving and a return; a searching apart from, even a fleeing from

God, and a rediscovery of his love; a homecoming. I see heaven as the ultimate homecoming. Sometimes tasting the depths, like the prodigal son in the pigpen eating husks, is the very thing we need to bring us to our senses, or to true humility.

In those times, then, where we feel God is nowhere, when he seems utterly absent and we feel we've been put out of his presence, out of his sight, our one determination – and I know mine rose up from the very depths of my spirit, though utterly without any sensation of hope – must be to nevertheless keep the Lord in our own line of vision. The writer of Hebrews understood how important it is to keep our eyes steadfastly on the Lord *"fixing our eyes on Jesus, the pioneer and perfecter of faith.." (Hebrews 12:2 partial).* He must be our focus at all times, good and bad, however absent he may seem. This is, perhaps always, but especially at the worst times in our spiritual lives, the very definition of faith. And lest we congratulate ourselves on our own faith if we are survivors of such darkness, we must remember that even our faith is a gift from God (Romans 12:3) and all our victories are won in Christ, who is the very embodiment of victory over hopelessness, obedient faith winning out over the darkness and uncertainty of a tortuous, lingering death.

The Reluctant Prophet

If overcoming, choosing the positive over the negative, keeping on going faithfully through troubles, is indeed one focus of a God-centred life, then Jonah's reluctance to go the distance – both literally and figuratively- followed by his reluctance to be the agent of God's mercy for Nineveh, asks important questions of us all. How much do we actually want the conversion of our enemies, or our friends for that matter? When we preach the gospel are we just going through the motions?

Can we be a little bit honest with our own unconscious failings of mercy and our fears of what the gospel succeeding in our lives might mean? What if *those* neighbours start coming to *my* church? We don't really want their type. What if so and so expects me to be nice to him once he's a Christian? What if that person gets into heaven now when they don't deserve it? These are the rotten thoughts we've all no doubt, albeit unconsciously for the most part, had flash through our minds.

Do we still not understand that it is not for us to decide, that as he told Moses, God will have mercy on whom he will have mercy, that we have not engineered nor deserved our salvation? The truth is, we don't deserve to be part of God's kingdom either. Of course the most wonderful expression of this is in the Parable Jesus tells about the vineyard workers (Matthew 20). This is a warning against what I call salvation smugness, which is sadly very prevalent in our churches today. God loves us and calls us into mercy through Christ, and we gladly accept it, mistaking it for a prize we have won, looking down on the sinners around us who've not had the sense or the wisdom to acknowledge Jesus. More fools them, we cry. Instead we should recognise the fact that we have been hugely blessed through no good of our own making and be eager to tell others they can have the same. It's a lot like the difference between sitting in a lifeboat congratulating oneself on one's ability to have been hauled aboard, whilst ignoring those in peril who are exactly where we were a few moments ago, instead of reaching towards them with outstretched arms knowing we were all in the water together and that there is room in the lifeboats for everyone.

There is a quote, often wrongly attributed to Nelson Mandela, which was actually penned by Marianne Williamson, used to often make me feel spiritually uncomfortable, though I find it hard to articulate exactly why.

"Our deepest fear is not that we are inadequate. Our deepest fear is that we are powerful beyond measure. It is our light, not our darkness that most frightens us. We ask ourselves, Who am

I to be brilliant, gorgeous, talented, fabulous? Actually, who are you not to be? You are a child of God. Your playing small does not serve the world. There is nothing enlightened about shrinking so that other people won't feel insecure around you. We are all meant to shine, as children do. We were born to make manifest the glory of God that is within us. It's not just in some of us; it's in everyone. And as we let our own light shine, we unconsciously give other people permission to do the same. As we are liberated from our own fear, our presence automatically liberates others."

I think that maybe it made me squirm because it can be read as individualistic, success-driven and more about us shining than letting God's light shine through us. But when we read it as people of true humility, there is a different kind of uncomfortable truth presenting itself. Because Jesus tells us in the Sermon on the Mount that there is no point hiding our lights, but that we must use them to guide others to God. I use it here to remind us that success and failure are both frightening in the field of preaching the gospel. We are frightened of being ineffective or inadequate and converting no-one, and we are equally scared of what might happen if people actually listened to us.

Perhaps both attitudes are leading us up the garden path towards ourselves instead of up God's path to him. If we are obedient to the Lord then the success or failure we observe is not our problem. Prophets of Old knew that the effect of God's words spoken through them, and God's actions done through them were all about him and their job was simply to obey. The very idea of success and failure is largely a western construct, perhaps especially so in the area of salvation. We seem to be ever driven by our market based, win or lose capitalist culture even in our religion. For a start, the great commission given by Jesus was to make disciples or followers, not converts. There is an important distinction. Disciples need to be looked after, taught, mentored, come alongside. Converts can be quickly persuaded and then left to their own devices, after all, they're saved, aren't they?

Secondly, the words we speak or the actions we perform may be simply planting a seed in someone's heart or mind. It may take years and many other conversations with others before this results in faith. Of course, we should be passionate about the gospel and loving towards all, but to make evangelism all about us is going about things the wrong way round. God can be trusted in this, as in all things. Hearing and obeying are more crucial than worrying about numbers. Jonah finds that his effectiveness is completely unhindered by his own bad attitude, reluctance and sulking; his own lack of compassion towards the people of Nineveh has no bearing on what the Lord does with his obedience.

God wants nothing more or less from us than this one thing: our yes. For what else is it that we think God needs and does not already have? As our true parent, he will love each child of his fiercely whether we return that love or not. It is true that he hopes to win our hearts and have us love him back, not because he needs our love, but because it is good for us to love him.

He wants your yes so that he can bless you, and the world through you. For if God has an undiluted "yes" from each of us, both to his goodness and his plans, then we shall have heaven on earth. Our yes will mean we can receive and channel his loving kindness. It makes us each, in both suffering and abundance, a conduit of grace.

Jonah had to travel approximately 500 miles overland to reach Nineveh. This would have been no easy or quick journey. He made it in the end out of sheer obedience, perhaps spurred on by the vow he had made in response to God's saving him. His salvation prompts him to go out to save others. This ought to be a model for us today. Our gratitude at being recipients of grace should be one of the things that motivates our outreach, not our feelings of obligation. But perhaps feelings of thankfulness give way to feelings of duty over such a long journey. Gratitude is after all, something that we humans struggle to maintain over any length of time, easily forgetting the Lord's goodness to us, as we see time and time again in the story of God's love affair with Israel. So if duty becomes one of the things Jonah is motivated by, perhaps it makes him bitter and resentful, as it often does us. Some of my friends would describe this as "hardened oughteries" and it can be cold-blooded as well as harmful to one's spiritual health.

If we think of his long difficult journey, of all he went through before that and the fact that Nineveh is a city of Assyrians – enemies to an Israelite prophet, perhaps we can begin to see why Jonah got angry when he felt he'd come all that way for what he saw as nothing. Of course the truth is that it was very much for something, the repentance of an entire city. Perhaps part of Jonah's frustration can be read as his knowing that God would save the city and let it survive and he felt that's what would have happened anyway if he hadn't come. Jonah fails to see the difference that the repentance of the city makes, that it allows for an eternal salvation as well as for an earthly relationship with God, both of which are far more precious than simply allowing them to carry on living. I have maintained for some years that the two most dangerous words in the English language are "us" and "them." Jonah doesn't want "them" saved. But we are not to put limits on God's compassion.

Perhaps Jonah doesn't see why he needed to come all that way, couldn't God have had compassion on the city and used someone else – someone already there to pass on the offer of repentance? But if we are part of God's chosen people then we must expect to be sent out with the good news. That was a prophetic mission in more ways than one if it shows Christians the way forward! We must trust too that God has his reasons for the seemingly (to us) strange ways he goes about things, and the choices that he makes. Could there have been a more reluctant messenger to Pharaoh than Moses, who makes every excuse under the sun not to go? Could there have been a better messenger to Pharaoh than Moses, when we look back? God knew how it would be.

More worryingly, especially as we can see by now that Jonah reflects many of our own faults, is the idea that the prophet feels his journey was wasted because he wanted the city to perish. This in fact, seems most likely given his outburst after the city is saved. Again, it's an illustration of what bitterness arises when we make our own judgments and when we decide who deserves salvation and who doesn't.

A Second Chance

When the Lord gives Jonah his instructions the second time, he words things differently. Knowing that Jonah will leap to his own conclusions about what is going to happen (which led him to decide not to bother the first time) the Lord wisely keeps his message for Nineveh close to his chest the second time around. Jonah can make fewer assumptions now and fewer excuses. He must choose simply either to obey or disobey, and given the vows he has made in the whale, he chooses to obey. God's message to Nineveh turns out to only consist, in translation anyway, as we already said, of only eight words. Perhaps part of Jonah's anger is that he came all that way to only say a few words. Part of his anger is prideful perhaps.

Those of us who preach or teach often spend a great deal of time, thought and effort preparing great long, erudite talks. Or at least that's what we want our congregations to think! But though preparation is wise, we must always be open to what God wants to say and how he wants to use us. Erudition is rarely the way to someone's heart. Instead of being pleased that so little effort was required on his part, Jonah would perhaps have liked to play out his role as respected prophet a little further, after all, he was expecting to have to spend three days preaching throughout the city. But no, the Lord's message was accepted instantaneously, the city repentant and Jonah left with nothing to do but wander off. No-one needed any explanation, no sermon, no detail. All they needed to know was that they were in trouble with God. A prophet proclaims that in forty more days, Nineveh will be overturned (Jonah 3:4) and their hearts are changed. How we ought to rejoice at an entire city being converted from godlessness to relationship with the Lord in an instant! And yet how likely is it that should any of us have been in Jonah's place that we would also have been hurt, angry and taken aback at how little we were needed. But the truth is that when God speaks, it is all that is necessary.

We embellish and extrapolate for our own sakes and do no good to anyone and sometimes, hard as it is to admit, all we are seeking to do is to enhance our own reputations. Please don't misunderstand me, we all need good, solid teaching, and our preachers are bound by tradition and contract to give us our money's worth. But when the Spirit moves, when the Lord speaks, we need to obey and then step back out of the way.

There is of course another reason for Jonah's anger. He is livid that the city has repented so easily because he was hoping God would judge them and send calamity. He was hoping it even against his own knowledge of God's character, as we saw in chapter 4 verse 2. Nineveh was a city of Assyrians and could be looked upon as Israel's enemies at this time. Jonah wanted to see fire and brimstone. How often are we like this too! "But Lord," our hearts (if not our voices) cry, "they are sinners!" How easily we forget that that's exactly who we are too!

God's mercies extend even to Israel's enemies and this is a lesson to Jonah that parallels his own salvation, though he cannot yet see it. If we accept God's mercies and grace for ourselves we need to be able to extend them to others and to be glad when they are accepted. This is all part and parcel of true forgiveness, and Jonah wasn't the first or last person to find this hard.

Jonah is angry to the point of wanting to die. This is some serious ire! I am imagining him in an anger management class as I write. How would he get on I wonder? But the Lord questions his right to be angry and instead of answering the question, Jonah does what many of us are also experts at. He sulks. Sulking is really what Jonah does best. He was essentially sulking on the ship as he tried to flee from God. But is sulking more than a bad habit?

Sulking is childish. It is another way of fleeing (Jonah's specialty) and it stinks of self-absorbency and self-pity. It is a failure to face something, in this case, to really address the question God is asking. Jonah and God both already know the answer to the question of course. They both know that Jonah has no right at all to be angry, but Jonah still *feels* angry and I don't think he knows what to do with that. Our emotions often rule us instead of helping us. Fortunately, God is merciful and understanding. God has every right to be angry and exasperated by Jonah, but he treats him with patience and keeps trying to teach him. There is a depth of relationship here that I find very touching. They do not see eye to eye, God and Jonah; but they know one another. Jonah knows what God is like and who he is, his description of God's character is quite beautiful, but it is also comic, because Jonah is angry at God for being so slow to anger, despite the fact that, in a delicious irony, which I happen to believe tickles God as much as it does us, that it is precisely that slowness to anger and that mercy that has saved Jonah's own skin and is the reason he continues to live and breathe.

Scorched

And the story of Jonah could so easily end there. But Jonah's mega sulk continues (and gives those of us with a penchant for sulking our own hopes that the Lord will be merciful to us as well). Jonah sits in the desert, sulking, and makes his own shelter. God provides an even better shelter for him in the form of the vine. God's shade and shelter are always so much better than our own.

When God takes his provision away and causes the sun to scorch and the wind to blow the heat and sand in Jonah's face, the prophet is again fiercely angry *"..I'm so angry I wish I were dead"* (4:9 partial). His anger seems to utterly consume him. His anger then is such that he can't contain it and is beyond his wits' end with rage. (more anger therapy sessions beckon).

Again, God patiently questions Jonah's anger. We are all of us built with a capacity for anger and we are right to be angry at injustice. If we have a warped view of our own importance in the scheme of things or of the injustices done to us or those we care about or indeed at the justice meted out to others, we can have a warped anger that rears its head at mercy. As we've noted, this is dealt with wonderfully in the parable Jesus tells about the vineyard workers who are angry when other workers are paid the same as they are for far less work (Matthew 20).

When we put up with a long-term problem, such as poverty, chronic sickness or disability, we can find ourselves, often understandably, thinking Jonah-like thoughts. We feel angry, let-down, fed up, everything in us screaming that this was not how it was supposed to play out, that this is not what we imagined "life in all its fullness" would be. We did not sign up for this! This is certainly how I often feel, especially when my depression rears its ugly head yet again, or I have a prolonged flare up of my illness. The unfairness of it can move us into a deep and destructive anger. Yes, I do think many of us can relate to Jonah's feelings. And yet, when we decided to worship this God, creator of heaven and earth, when we vowed to follow his Son, Jesus, whose life was one of sorrows, we did sign up for this.

One way I believe the modern Protestant Church lets its members down is by denying or underplaying the truth that we would have troubles, that we would need to fight physical and spiritual battles daily. The Scriptures are full of this truth, and our sermons frequently empty of it. No wonder we can feel scorched so often, shaking our fists at the Lord, and hanging our blistered heads, wondering perhaps what we did wrong to deserve such misfortune, instead of seeing it as part of a far larger picture.

Jonah feels more able to answer God's question now, perhaps because he's done sulking, more likely because his anger is just bursting out of him. We get angry about things that affect us directly and up close, don't we? With Jonah it is the vine, with us as well as the huge long-term difficulties we've spoken about it might well also be when our laptop stops working or we're fobbed off by a call centre or more seriously when we are injured or cheated on. Injustice hurts more when it is up close and personal. At such times the bigger picture eludes us and the smaller, intimate injustice looms large. This is our egos looming large as well and it can be a mark of our own selfishness, however understandable. Things that hurt us, hurt more. Unlike God, who feels and knows all pain, our capacity for compassion is centred very much on the things we have experienced ourselves, which is why our wounds tend to mirror the places we can bring the most healing to others.

Experiences of wounding can leave us feeling scorched like Jonah's poor head. We smart and we are too busy hurting to learn any lessons that the pain is trying to teach us. But if we listen carefully within those difficult places, and concentrate more on the Lord than on our own anger at the seeming injustice we have suffered, we may find that our compassion is being stretched and our hearts enlarged to include love for people, cities, enemies or animals that we had not thought to consider before.

Those of us who have suffered with it, may find that we continue to be dogged by depression on and off our whole lives. Just because we avoided suicide, or conquered suicidal thoughts, does not always mean that we have been miraculously healed. We may revisit our depths in painful ways now and then throughout the rest of our days. This is normal, and part I think of the way that our difficulties continue to test and refine us. Such experiences might be thought of as similar to St Paul's "thorn in the flesh," for in truth, there are many things that continue to plague us and which we will not necessarily be free of until we arrive home. When we are in these deep, difficult places, it is our whale songs, and our knowledge of who God is, that will continue to give us hope and deliverance.

Disaster and Salvation

Ra'ah is a Hebrew word used in Jonah ten times and used variously to mean: evil; disaster; discomfort and displeasure. It is the word used not only for the evil being perpetrated in Nineveh (1:2, 3:8) but also for Jonah's own discomfort in the desert (4:6) and for his displeasure at the withering of the vine (4:1).

Evil is perhaps then in the eye of the beholder to some extent and is a matter of perspective. It is evil in Jonah's eyes that the vine died, it is evil done to him that his comfort is taken away from him, yet he fails to see that it is a microcosmic picture of how he wants Nineveh's story to unfold. He does not want mercy extended to them, yet he blusters in rage when mercy is removed from his own head. To give Jonah some compassionate understanding here we need to remember that at this moment he was quite literally hot-headed! How often do we speak angrily in the heat of the moment, even to God? I know I do!

When Jonah is in distress from the heat, God appoints a vine to save him from that distress. Jonah rejoices in his salvation from the heat, God destroys the vine, Jonah sees the destruction of the vine as calamitous – because it is done (he feels) to him personally. He fails to see that he is the vine that was sent to save Nineveh from its distress, its impending disaster. Instead of rejoicing in that role he cannot see beyond his own situation. One of the things I believe God wants Jonah to understand is that if he destroyed Nineveh's vine, its salvation, and relented to the prophet's view of things and sent judgment, that this would be wrong, and more importantly against God's merciful character. If Jonah is going to grasp this, he may well only be able to do so in relation to himself, which is what I believe the episode of the vine and the worm is all about. Without this happening he will never be able to put himself in the position of the people of the city or see his role in things clearly. The reluctant prophet only imagines that God has made him look foolish, he does not see that he has been the means of bringing the Living God's salvation to a huge number of people and that this is good! He wants the vine for himself, but not for anyone else. How often are we guilty of the same misperception?

Most interestingly ra'ah is used as the evil that God sees Nineveh turning away from as well as the disaster he relents from sending. (3:10) So evil/disaster can be human (sin) appointed or God appointed. The good news is that people can repent of the first and God can then relent of the second. Our repentance, our turning from sin to God is still the key principle in forgiveness and allows God to remove the punishment for that sin. In repenting, we rid ourselves of two evils, two lots of disaster.

What triggers this repentance? Well, God does, as always, in his mercy and his infinite patience. He wants our freedom. He wants relationship with the people of Nineveh, so he sends Jonah. Jonah preaches a sermon consisting of eight words in English and I believe only five in Hebrew: *"Forty more days and Nineveh will be overturned."* (Jonah 3:4) and the King issues a proclamation of repentance, the people of the city are already in agreement with his orders because they also respond to the prophet's warning.

Several things are striking about this scenario. One is how much God is in control of events. His plans for restoration may be delayed if one of his chosen people disobeys instructions for a while, but never changed. The outcome was always going to be the salvation of Nineveh. God is the author of the whole plot, it is he who notices the evil present in the city (its evil has come up before him) it is his plan that is put into action to help them turn away from that evil and it is his goodness and mercy that allows the city's repentance to be the means of not only avoiding punishment but of bringing relationship with the Living God into their hitherto pagan lives.

Second is how God uses Jonah's disobedience to not only teach Jonah, although how much he's really learned by the end of the history is doubtful, but also to save the pagan sailors on the ship to Joppa, and who knows how many more souls through the witness they will have to tell others on their travels, but also, in parallel to that, he uses what Jonah does to teach us and the generations of believers before and after us. It wouldn't be much of a tale in our human perspective if Jonah had gone straight to Nineveh and preached, although this would have also been amazing, but the need for narrative that God has built into us in order, I believe, to help us understand things of the kingdom better, responds to the tale of Jonah and his attempts to flee his destiny.

Jonah's tale screams out the truth that God uses even our mistakes and our disobedience in his plans. This should not be an encouragement to us to be disobedient, but it should encourage us that God always has things in hand, always works for good, is the master of turning around situations that seem hopeless to our human eyes, and also that if he has plans, we cannot thwart them. We can to some extent perhaps change plans he has for us, we can delay them and we can be resolutely stubborn or disobedient and that will have consequences for us. We may find ourselves at some point at the bottom of the sea, or in the belly of a whale. We can make life exceedingly difficult for ourselves. But this does not change God's plans and all of it can be used by him.

For myself I find it tremendously encouraging to know, having been through those times of terrible darkness, that they will not be for nothing, because now that I am struggling to be on the same page as God, instead of struggling against him, my past is also something that has been given over to him and he *will* use it, and use it for good. It is, I believe, going to benefit others and the kingdom and maybe even me. But it is all included, it is all useable. It is all God's.

When I think of the repentance of Nineveh, of a people God describes as not knowing their left hand from their right (which means, presumably that they do not know God, that they are morally and spiritually ignorant), and of how quick they are to recognise their own sin, and to recognise the voice of God speaking through an Israelite prophet, someone they might have well regarded as an enemy, what strikes and saddens me is comparing this with how the world, particularly in the west, is able to look straight at its own sin without flinching, revelling in it and maybe even calling it freedom, and our complete failure to recognise not only sin for what it is, but our failure to hear the voice of God calling out to us as it does constantly, not only to repentance and to the joy of relationship with God, but doing so through the tremendous gift of his own son, Jesus Christ. This is the strongest love call that the world could receive and yet it is so often not only ignored but cast aside and even ridiculed.

How many times today does a prophet or person of God speak eight words (in translation anyway) and bring a city to its knees? How have we become so deaf to the voice of God and blind to our own revolting practices? Has the cacophony of sin and wanton desires grown so ubiquitous that there is no frequency on which God can reach us? Well the short answer to that is no, because God can do anything. But whilst His words still achieve what they intend, and never return to him void, the human race has become far more in character like Jonah in chapter one of his story. We have to be dragged to the bottom of the seabed, to the roots of the mountains, more often than not, before we can see that God is the only way out.

We have to get ourselves into such messes of disobedience and stubborn refusal that we find we are knocking on spiritual death's door before we can find the one who spends all his time looking for us. Our moral compasses are adrift and our desires are skewed and our understanding of the world and of ourselves is rewarded when it is based on egocentricity and individualism.

The good news in this is that we are still moved by goodness, kindness, community, sacrifice, all things of God, loving kindness, mercy and unfailing love, perhaps particularly by unconditional love that keeps on enduring, because these things are so clearly foreign to us now that they speak of the supernatural kingdom. But the bad news is that our hearts are hardened, selfish and apathetic. We are hard to reach. We are a tough crowd.

Perhaps as I've already intimated, in this hard-hearted world, loving actions do in fact speak louder than a prophet's words. But always the flow of the Holy Spirit should guide us in this; we should look to her to know what is most appropriate for the person or people in front of us. Leading someone to the Lord is likely to be a longer process now with many more steps and more people along the way. But the eight words you are moved to speak to someone, however unlikely it may seem to you, may be the ones that finally bring that person to their knees before God. You are not likely to see that result; we don't fall to our knees so easily these days. But if you are given over to be used of God, the Spirit will lead you. Always trust the Lord, never the world.

Compassion

Whilst God's holy prophet struggles to care about the inhabitants of Nineveh, the pagans in the book put him to shame with their compassion and *are* concerned about people perishing. The sailors on the boat to Joppa do not want to throw Jonah into the raging sea, they try to find another way. The King of Nineveh does not want his people to perish. In particular, God does not want anyone to perish:

"For I take no pleasure in the death of anyone, declares the Sovereign LORD. Repent and live!" **(Ezekiel 18:32)**

"The Lord is not slow in keeping his promise, as some understand slowness. Instead he is patient with you, not wanting anyone to perish, but everyone to come to repentance." (2 Peter 3:9)

The Lord wants to save Nineveh, the sailors *and* Jonah. And he does. But Jonah seldom cares about something or someone perishing, the first time seems to be caring finally about himself at the bottom of the sea. I'm not convinced in the previous storm that he's that bothered about perishing because he is still fleeing from God down in the bowels of the ship, he is still hiding *and* he tells the sailors to throw him in the sea, rather than throwing himself in. So, I think he is at that point in his story just obsessed with being against God. Once his life is actually at the point of being taken away from him on the seabed and after going through a truly terrifying experience, he sees that he needs the Rescuer and does care about not perishing. He has then faced death and chosen life as we talked about earlier. It is likely, if we are trying to be fair to Jonah, that it is compassion as well as resignation that causes him to tell the sailors to throw him overboard: *"I know that it is my fault that this great storm has come upon you."* (Jonah 1:12 partial)

The only other time he appears to worry about something dying is when he is angry at the plant perishing, but really only for his own sake again. And his reaction is once more to sulk – he tells God he wants to die. He has thrown back in God's face the gift of life he's been given twice. Nor does he want anyone else to have it! But God tries to reason with him. Why, I wonder, does God mention the cattle (or simply animals in some translations) in his final question?

"And should not I pity Nineveh, that great city, in which there are more than 120,000 persons who do not know their right hand from their left, and also much cattle?"

(4:11 ESV)

Maybe if Jonah can care about a vine, he might care about animals. But the reality is that as Jonah doesn't care about the vine, but only about the shelter it gave him, it is not true compassion. So perhaps he can be moved by the plight of cattle because he can see their innocence? Or perhaps he is one of those people who simply does not like people. A lot of people, particularly those who have been hurt badly, find it easier to give their affection and trust to animals than to people and maybe God knows Jonah's heart is like this. We don't know where Jonah's hurt stems from, but God does. And he ends Jonah's story or at least, what we know of it, with a challenge, both to his prophet and to us. What do we care about?

Can we care about "them" as well as "us", when to God we are all part of his creation? Perhaps mentioning the cattle is also an inclusive point, God is telling us that these are people just like us who care for their cattle just as we do. God cares for them, both the people and their livestock. So then, should we.

We don't get to hear Jonah's reply. I don't think any other book of the Bible ends with God asking us a question. It truly is left up in the air. As a narrative device, this not only gives the Lord the last word, but it also begs an answer not only from Jonah, but from all those who read it. Clearly it is something the writer of the book wants everyone to consider. What is worth caring about? If God cares about foreigners, about those who are not like us and don't even know him, can we do the same? If God cares about the lives of animals, shouldn't we follow his lead? If this is a God who is driven first and foremost by compassion, then this should be a byword for how we look at the world, how we live our lives, and particularly how we characterise ourselves as his worshippers. Because if we serve a God of mighty love who has compassion for all living creatures, then that love and mercy is also our motivation. Hundreds of years before Jesus said that all of the Law of Moses hangs upon the love of God and the love of ourselves and our neighbours, Jonah's story confirms that love is indeed at the very heart of the character of God.

Conclusion

I may be contrary, but it gives me hope that an Old Testament prophet can slip back to his old, bad habits so quickly. It was sulking that got Jonah sent to the bottom of the sea but even though he has not yet learnt his lesson – even after God has saved him in a miraculous manner – God has not given up on him. God still talks to Jonah with compassion and in the hope that he will begin to comprehend. I know from my own experience that this is all part of God's wonderful patience and understanding. He knows that spiritually, and more often than not in these modern God-forsaking (it is certainly not God who has forsaken *us*) times, emotionally and psychologically too, we are little more than toddlers. We will bang our little fists against his knees no matter how many times he picks us up and places us where we need to be. We will throw our food against the wall and he will continue to provide it for us, at whatever cost.

Perhaps then, we might remember that the best thing we can do when we are pulled back down to those seabed places, is to sing our whale song. To let the truths we discovered (or maybe which discovered us) in the darkness rise up once more and be our road to Christ the Redeemer. We must know that healing can be just as much a constant feature of our lives as suffering. So many Kingdom things are process and are about becoming, about beginning, with the finalisation something we can visualise but not yet see.

This is how I feel about my own time in the depths, which continue to teach and mould me. There is less and less pain attached to those memories as time goes on, but it has taken many years to see that softening. And there is more and more strength for me in the truth that God loved me through it and loves me through each day now in my weakness, as well. My whale song continues to sustain me in the raw power of what I knew when there was nothing beneath me, no false platitudes held true, nothing but the Truth itself, the utterly constant power at the centre of the universe, Love, was all that remained.

It was to that Love I turned that day, without feeling it, and to that same Love I have returned day after day ever since, with more and more love to give of my own to the Living God who created heaven and earth. The truth of love grows over time, and the knowing of it, and the giving of it. That is the song that I sing, the song that gives me life every time that I re-choose it.

God has the last word in Jonah's story, and this gives us as the readers, and fellow students of the nature of God and his creation, hope that Jonah maybe hears and understands the question at last. It is one we all need to consider. The scale and scope of God's mercy and compassion can never be understood by us, but we would do well to remember it and emulate it when we can.

Jonah gives those of us who are slow on the uptake and who look to our own needs too much, those of us who are quick to judge and hard of heart sometimes, those of us who desperately want to see justice but who too often misunderstand grace; he gives all of us hope that the dialogue with the Lord continues despite our faults and that he is a God of compassion and humour and mercy.

The book of Jonah gives us hope that where and when we feel we've "missed it" whether through our own fault or no, that God is a God who is not only comfortable with course changes, he plots them with ease and makes the winding journeys that result bring forth their own fruit. God even uses Jonah's recalcitrance to teach and console millions of people through scripture. It reminds me of the saying, "If you can't be a good example, be a horrible warning." But Jonah knows God well, and who can say in his place we would behave any better or see any deeper than the surface of things.

Be encouraged. Nothing in the story fazes the Living God: not deliberate disobedience, not cities full of wickedness, not boatloads of idolaters, not sulking prophets, not long journeys, not fits of anger, not the deep hurt of being constantly misunderstood. On the contrary, the wicked city, the sulking prophet and the boatload of unbelievers: all are saved by the goodness and mercy of our God. Let us put our hope in him and praise his name.

Questions for Reflection

How do we discern a calling from God?

Have you ever felt called to do something that you *really* did not want any part of?

Did you ever feel sure something was going to go a different way to how you wanted it go, but that it needed to be done anyway?

If so, how did you reconcile yourself to the outcome?

Have you ever tried to flee from God? Do you think that it is possible?

Where and how might we hide ourselves from the Lord?

If someone from another country asked who you were, how would you describe yourself? Would God come into your definition?

What storms have there been in your life, and how have you weathered them?

What lessons might you take forwards from thinking about that?

Have you ever felt "hedged" or "barred" in by God? What kind of prayers can we say at such a time?

What have been your trapped on the seabed with seaweed round your head moments in life so far?

How did you deal with them? How did God help you deal with them? Do you feel perhaps that he didn't? Why might it seem that way?

Have you ever felt that God rescued you? Is there anything in your life now that has you so trapped you feel that it's about time God sent a "great fish" to help you out?

Are God's plans for us always good? How does self-sacrifice, hardship and suffering fit into them?

Have you ever been so angry at God that, like Jonah, in the heat of the moment you wished you were dead?

Do you think that you had any right to feel like that?

What arouses your compassion?

What in your life do you think arouses God's compassion?

What might he say to you out of his great mercy?

Final Prayer

Lord, when we find ourselves in need of rescue, come save us.

When we are disobedient, show us our foolishness, and remain patient with us, as any loving parent with their small child.

When we don't know how to proceed, show us where the next foothold is, and make a way, even if it is the tenth course change in a day.

When we run and hide, never stop chasing after us, sweet lover of our souls.

Be with us in our scorchings, and when we rage against life's unfairness.

When we are angry, keep engaging us with your questions about grace.

Father, when we are in danger, or sunk to great depths of misery, come lift us up.

At these dark times, let your mercy and compassion meet us like a great fish, poised to carry us to safe harbours.

Set our feet there on solid rock and send us gently on our way with you always beside us.

Amen.

About the Author

Keren Dibbens-Wyatt is a mystic in the Christian tradition with a passion for prayer and creativity. She writes to encourage others into knowing the Lord more intimately as well as to share the poetic ponderings of her heart. A Christian for over 30 years, Keren has been answering a call into a deep prayer relationship with the Lord for half that time, practising centring prayer and contemplation daily. She is no stranger to difficulties as she has had disabling M.E. for two decades, often being housebound or using a wheelchair.

Keren has an honours degree in English and European Literature. She lives in South East England with her poet husband and their slightly deranged black and white cat. She writes prayers, poetry, blogs, theology, prose-poems, short stories for adults and fiction for older children. Publications include her book of meditations *Garden of God's Heart*, a handbook for the edification of Christian women called *Positive Sisterhood* and an e-book of prayers *Christian Prayers for the World*. She writes regularly for Godspace (the blog of Mustard Seed Associates) and guest posts on spiritual matters for other Christian sites. She has recently discovered a talent for painting in pastels which she enjoys immensely, and other interests when she has the energy include reading, enjoying nature, photography and crocheting things that inevitably come out wonky.

You can connect with Keren at her website
www.kerendibbenswyatt.com

Printed in Great Britain
by Amazon